LET'S DANCE!

Modern and Contemporary

CHERRY LAKE PRESS
Ann Arbor, Michigan

by Joyce Markovics

Cherry Lake Press

Published in the United States of America by
Cherry Lake Publishing Group
Ann Arbor, Michigan
www.cherrylakepublishing.com

Reading Adviser: Beth Walker Gambro, MS Ed., Reading Consultant, Yorkville, IL

Content Adviser: Justin Wingenroth, dancer and owner/director of The Dance Conservatory, Cortland Manor, New York

Book Designer: Ed Morgan, Bowerbird Books

Photo Credits: © photo-nuke/Shutterstock, cover and title page; © Master1305/Shutterstock, 5; © PeopleImages.com-Yuri A/Shutterstock, 6; © Sun Shock/Shutterstock, 7; © Pressmaster/Shutterstock, 8-9; Wikimedia Commons, 11, 12, and 15 bottom; © Album/Fine Art Images/Newscom, 13; © Album/Metropolitan Museum of Art, NY/Newscom, 14; © Arnold Genthe/Heritage Art/Heritage Images AiWire/Newscom, 15 top; © Arnold Genthe/Heritage Art/Heritage Images AiWire/Newscom, 16; © Album/Fine Art Images/Newscom, 17; © RDELALANDE/SIPA/Newscom, 18-19; Library of Congress, Prints and Photographs Division, 20; © akg-images/Newscom, 21; Library of Congress, Prints and Photographs Division, Van Vechten Collection, 22; © BACAUSA.COM/Newscom, 23; © lev radin/Shutterstock, 24; Trib LaPrade/Wikimedia Commons, 25; © Master1305/Shutterstock, 27.

Cherry Lake Press is an imprint of Cherry Lake Publishing Group.

Library of Congress Cataloging-in-Publication Data has been filed and is available at catalog.loc.gov

Printed in the United States of America

Contents

It's SHOWTIME!

"Dance is the only art in which we ourselves are the stuff of which it is made."
—Ted Shawn

A single dancer is barefoot on stage. Wearing a **leotard**, the dancer lifts her leg until it extends above her head. As she releases her leg, her body then folds. Fast violin music begins. The dancer raises her upper body and arms. Then she leaps high into the air. All of her movements come from her core. Another dancer joins her. On his toes, he spins toward the center of the stage. The two dancers **intertwine** their bodies and separate. The pace of the music slows down. In **sync**, the dancers raise their arms. They bend their knees, sinking closer to the floor. The performers show strength, control, and beauty. The audience is filled with wonder and excitement.

Modern dancers are often trained in many different styles of dance.

What Is MODERN and CONTEMPORARY DANCE?

"Dance is the hidden language of the soul, of the body."
—Martha Graham

Dance is an art form that has many different styles. Modern dance and contemporary dance are two of those styles. Both styles center around how dancers express and move their bodies. The movements may tell stories, **evoke** emotions, or communicate ideas. Other times, the movements themselves are the sole focus of a dance. For example, modern **choreographer** Merce Cunningham thought that movement should be appreciated for what it is. In other words, dance itself was the subject of his work.

Modern and contemporary dancers express themselves through movement.

Both modern dance and contemporary dance represent a break from the past. Ballet, for example, is known for structure. There are a set number of steps. And ballet dancers follow many rules. Modern and contemporary dances, however, are much freer and more fluid. In ballet, dancers wear pointe shoes and tutus. Modern and contemporary dancers are often barefoot and wear loose costumes. This allows them to move more easily.

A dancer extends his leg with flexed instead of pointed toes. Pointed toes are more characteristic of ballet.

Modern and contemporary choreographers use steps from ballet, jazz, African, and other dance styles.

There are many similarities between modern dance and contemporary dance. So, what are the differences? Modern dance was created in the late 1800s and early 1900s. Several trailblazing dancers and choreographers turned it into a popular dance. They came up with their own teaching methods and **techniques**. Some, like Martha Graham, changed the way people moved their bodies and thought about dance.

Contemporary dance, on the other hand, blends modern dance with other styles, such as jazz and hip-hop. Choreographer Ray Leeper describes it this way: "Contemporary is anything current. It's a **fusion** of many techniques." Many times, instead of following rules, contemporary dance breaks rules. As it does, new steps are invented.

Music can be an important part of both dance styles. The music can help guide the dancers' bodies. Or the dance can be performed in silence or to other sounds.

Both styles of dance connect people around the world. Dance cuts across **cultures**. It's also an important link to the past! Did you know that dance is one of the oldest art forms? Cave paintings from 10,000 years ago show dancing. Later, the ancient Egyptians danced. Early peoples in Asia and other parts of the world danced, too. They danced during **ceremonies** and also as part of their daily lives. Over time, dance changed. It **evolved** into an art. Dance allowed people to use their imaginations and to express their thoughts and feelings. The creators of modern dance and contemporary dance changed the art form. Let's take a closer look at the history of their work!

Dance is an expression of many things, including history, culture, and emotion.

Shiva is an important god in the religion of Hinduism. He's often shown dancing. This statue is around 1,000 years old.

A Brief History

"I wanted to create a new form of art."
—Loie Fuller

Modern dance can be traced to the late 1800s in Europe. A Swiss music teacher named Émile Jacques-Dalcroze wanted his students to connect to the music they were playing. He sought to create more "communication between brain and body." So, he taught his pupils musical concepts through movement. He called this system eurhythmics. Many dancers took notice of what Émile was doing. They saw value in his approach.

Émile Jacques-Dalcroze

These dancers included Rudolf Laban, another European. Rudolf was interested in how the body moves in a space. He choreographed large dances called "movement choirs." Rudolf wanted dance to move beyond the **confines** of ballet. He also wanted dance to find "its own terms of expression."

Dancers trained in Rudolf Laban's eurhythmics technique.

Early modern dance is commonly called expressionist dance. It was also known as the art of movement.

In 1890 in America, dancer Loie Fuller shocked the world. Born in Illinois, she was a natural performer from a young age. As an adult, Loie was best known for her Serpentine Dance. In it, she wore a **billowing** dress with long sleeves. When she danced, Loie spun around and twisted her arms. Colored lights lit up the dress. Loie looked like a giant moth fluttering its wings. No one had ever seen a dance like hers before. It embraced "the soul and the senses at the same time," said Loie. Her original work drew crowds. And it inspired other modern dance **pioneers**, including Isadora Duncan.

For a time, Loie Fuller was known as the most famous dancer in the world.

Isadora disliked ballet as a child in California. So, she taught herself how to dance. Isadora preferred more natural movements and dancing barefoot. "You do not play the piano with gloves on," she once said. When she became a performer, she wore loose dresses that allowed greater movement of her body. She saw movement as the **essence** of dance. In 1904, she founded a dance school to share her style with students.

Isadora Duncan dancing

Isadora Duncan called dance an "expression of the human spirit." She performed for audiences around the world.

Ruth St. Denis danced into her eighties. At that time, she said, "I move with remembered beauty."

Ruth St. Denis was another dancer who helped develop modern dance. Inspired by Asian art, she wove Indian, Chinese, Japanese, and other styles into her dance. In 1914, she married her dance partner, Ted Shawn. Together, they formed the Denishawn school and company. They encouraged their students to create "music **visualizations**" with their bodies. The school became a foundation of modern dance. And it **nurtured** a new **generation** of dancers.

One of Denishawn's star performers was Martha Graham. But Martha wanted more from dance. She believed that dance should communicate emotion. So, in the 1920s, she branched out on her own. She came up with her own dance technique based on **contracting** and releasing the muscles. Known for partnering with artists, designers, and musicians, she wowed audiences with her moving performances. Her vision had a powerful and long-lasting impact on modern dance.

Martha Graham is called the "mother of modern dance." Her company continues to influence dance of all kinds today.

Doris Humphrey was another founder of modern dance. She danced with the Denishawn company and then formed her own. Her technique was centered around balance and falling.

Other dancers followed in Martha's footsteps. Merce Cunningham, who danced in her company, was greatly influenced by her. But he had a different approach to dance. Martha saw emotion in movement. In contrast, Merce believed that movement is simply movement. He wanted viewers to focus on the dancing itself. Also, his technique looked more like ballet. His dancers often lifted or extended their arms and legs.

Merce introduced another new element into his work—chance. Sometimes, he would ask an audience member to flip a coin. The coin toss would decide the dancers' movements. Other times, Merce's dancers found out the music they would be performing to at the last minute. Merce's method transformed modern dance. And the people who came after him further changed it.

A dance choreographed by Merce Cunningham

Merce's partner in life and work was **avant-garde** musician John Cage. They **collaborated** on many dances together.

Famous Dancers

"You dance because you have to."
—Katherine Dunham

There were other **innovators** who made their mark on modern and contemporary dance. Katherine Dunham was part of this group. She studied African and Caribbean dance and culture. Katherine used the techniques she learned to form her own dance company. In the process, she helped shape modern dance. Like Katherine, Pearl Primus celebrated African dance. She saw dance as a way to fight for justice in the world. As a solo performer, she was known for her explosive energy. Her work greatly influenced other dancers.

Katherine Dunham has been called the "queen mother of Black dance."

Pearl Primus (left center) was born in Trinidad, an island in the Caribbean. In addition to being a dancer and choreographer, she was a scholar.

Lester Horton was working at the same time as Katherine and Pearl. However, he was inspired by Native American dances. Lester trained some incredible dancers, including Alvin Ailey. He was also one of the first white choreographers to include Black dancers in his company. "For Lester, his art was much more important than the color of a dancer's skin," Alvin wrote.

Alvin Ailey was born in Texas in 1931. He joined Lester Horton's dance company in 1942. When Lester died, Alvin took over. In 1958, Alvin formed his own company, which included mostly Black dancers. The Alvin Ailey American Dance Theater performed works by Katherine and Pearl. Alvin was also a choreographer. "I'm searching for truth in movement," he said.

Alvin Ailey as a young dancer

An Alvin Ailey American Dance Theater performance

Alvin strongly believed that dance belongs to all people. "Dance is for everybody," he said. "I believe that the dance came from the people and that it should always be delivered back to the people." Education was another big part of Alvin's mission. He helped bring dance to inner-city children. Alvin died in 1989. Today, he's considered one of the most important leaders in the history of dance.

Revelations **is one of Alvin Ailey's most famous dances. "I wanted to explore Black culture," he said. Alvin also wanted to honor "the memories of my parents, uncles, and aunts."**

Get Moving!

"No artist is ahead of his time. He is his time."
—Martha Graham

Alvin Ailey paved the way for a new generation of contemporary creators, including Kyle Abraham. Kyle seeks to bring Black and queer stories to the stage. He says his choreography "lives in the reality of my experiences and the cultural work that still needs to be done." Kyle also produces works for other contemporary dance companies. These include Paul Taylor, Bill T. Jones and Arnie Zane, and Kevin Wynne.

Kyle Abraham's dance company is called A.I.M.

AXIS Dance Company has a distinct mission. They showcase the beauty of difference. The company collaborates with people with and without disabilities. Some of their dancers use wheelchairs or crutches or are missing limbs. AXIS's goal is to challenge how dance and disability are viewed.

An AXIS Dance Company performance

Michaela Taylor is an exciting young dancer and choreographer. She combines contemporary technique with hip-hop.

"The most unique thing in the world is you."
—Alvin Ailey

No matter the style, every dancer has a unique story. Whenever they dance, they're sharing parts of themselves. They're also honoring the dancers that came before them. But you don't have to be a **professional** to dance. A person of any age and ability can join in! Taking a class is a terrific way to learn different techniques. It's also a wonderful way to stay fit. In addition to its physical benefits, dance can decrease stress. Dance also brings people together. Finally, it's an outlet for creativity. "The creative process is not controlled by a switch you can simply turn on or off," said Alvin Ailey. "It's with you all the time." So get out there, get moving—and let's dance!

Ohad Naharin is a dance innovator from Israel. He created a dance style called Gaga, which is known for open, twisting, and floating movements.

Seeing a performance is yet another way to experience modern and contemporary dance.

Learn to DANCE

Here's how to perform a basic modern dance step called a fan kick. Remember to move your body freely.

Step 1: Stand with your feet parallel and about as wide as your hips.

Step 2: Shift your weight to your left leg.

Step 3: Lift your right leg up and over to the side, making a half circle in the air.

Step 4: Bring your leg down and place it next to your standing leg.

Step 5: Now, shift your weight to your right leg.

Step 6: Lift your left leg up and over to the side in a half circle.

Step 7: Bring your leg down next to your standing leg.

Congrats, you just performed a double fan kick!

Glossary

avant-garde (uh-vahnt-GAHRD) very advanced or cutting edge

billowing (BIL-oh-ing) rising up, or rolling like waves

ceremonies (SER-uh-moh-neez) events that mark a special occasion

choreographer (kor-ee-AHG-ruh-fer) a person who creates the steps and moves for a dance performance

collaborated (kuh-LAB-uh-ray-tuhd) worked together on something

confines (kon-FYNZ) the limits of something

contracting (KON-trakt-ing) tightening a body part

cultures (KUHL-churz) the customs, ideas, art, and traditions that make up people's ways of life

essence (ES-uhns) the basic nature of something

evoke (ih-VOHK) to bring to mind

evolved (ih-VOLVD) developed over time

fusion (FYOO-zhuhn) a mixture of different styles

generation (jen-uh-RAY-shuhn) a group of people born around the same time

innovators (IN-uh-vay-turz) people that introduce something new or do something for the first time

intertwine (in-ter-TWAHYN) to twist together

leotard (LEE-uh-tahrd) a close-fitting one-piece garment made of a stretchy fabric

nurtured (NUR-cherd) supported and encouraged

pioneers (pye-uh-NEERZ) the first people to do something

professional (pruh-FESH-uh-nuhl) a person who gets paid to do something as a job rather than just for fun

sync (SINGK) two or more things moving at the same time

techniques (tek-NEEKS) skillful ways of doing something

visualizations (vih-zhoo-wuh-luh-ZAY-shuhs) mental images of something

Read More

BOOKS

Lanier, Wendy Hinote. *Modern Dance*. Lake Elmo, MN: Focus Readers, 2017.

Marisco, Kate. *Dancer*. Ann Arbor, Michigan: Cherry Lake Press, 2012.

Rooyackers, Paul. *101 Dance Games for Children*. Alameda, CA: Hunter House Publishing, 1996.

Learn More Online

WEBSITES

Explore these online sources with an adult:

Britannica: Modern Dance

Foundations Dance Collective: What Is Contemporary Dance?

The Institute for Arts Integration and STEAM: The History of Modern Dance

Index

About the Author

Joyce Markovics has written hundreds of children's books. She wholeheartedly thanks Justin Wingenroth for his expert help with this series. Joyce and Justin urge everyone to get up and dance!